# PIRATES *of the* CARIBBEAN
## DEAD MAN'S CHEST

Adapted by
IRENE TRIMBLE

Based on the screenplay written by
TED ELLIOTT & TERRY ROSSIO
Based on characters created by
TED ELLIOTT & TERRY ROSSIO
and STUART BEATTIE and JAY WOLPERT

Based on Walt Disney's
PIRATES OF THE CARIBBEAN

Produced by
JERRY BRUCKHEIMER

Directed by
GORE VERBINSKI

Level 3

Retold by Karen Holmes
Series Editors: Andy Hopkins and Jocelyn Potter

**Pearson Education Limited**
Edinburgh Gate, Harlow,
Essex CM20 2JE, England
and Associated Companies throughout the world.

ISBN: 978-1-4058-6773-3

This edition first published by Pearson Education Ltd 2008

5  7  9  10  8  6

Set in 11/14pt Bembo
Printed in China
SWTC/05

The authors have asserted their moral rights in accordance
with the Copyright Designs and Patents Act 1988

Produced for the publishers by Ken Vail Graphic Design

Published by Pearson Education Limited in association with
Penguin Books Ltd, and both companies being subsidiaries of Pearson PLC

# *Contents*

**page**

# Introduction

*The moon was high above a dark ocean. A stone prison stood above a beach. A group of guards carried six wooden boxes to the prison wall and threw them into the ocean below.*

*Suddenly, there was a gunshot inside one of the boxes. An arm reached through the newly made hole and opened the box. It was Captain Jack Sparrow, the smartest pirate who ever sailed the ocean.*

Jack Sparrow, pirate captain of the *Black Pearl*, is back in a new adventure, with Will Turner, Elizabeth Swann, and Commodore Norrington. This time, everybody is searching the Caribbean for an important prize—a chest belonging to the terrible Captain Davy Jones.

In their last adventure, Captain Sparrow's chief officer, Barbossa, stole the *Black Pearl*. Because of an old curse, Barbossa and the other pirates could never die. Barbossa attacked Port Royal and took away Elizabeth, the governor's daughter, but she was saved by Jack and Will Turner, the son of another pirate, Bootstrap Bill. Jack and Will stole a British ship, and followed the *Black Pearl* to the pirates' island, *Isla de Muerta*. Commodore Norrington followed them. When the curse was finally broken, Jack killed Barbossa. Will then saved Jack from Commodore Norrington. Norrington wanted to marry Elizabeth, but she chose Will. In trouble after Jack's escape, Norrington left Port Royal.

And now, at the beginning of *Pirates of the Caribbean: Dead Man's Chest*, Captain Jack Sparrow is in prison again.

The first *Pirates of the Caribbean* movie, *The Curse of the Black Pearl*, was made in 2003 with Johnny Depp as Captain Jack Sparrow, Orlando Bloom as Will Turner, and Keira Knightley as Elizabeth Swann. The second movie, *Dead Man's Chest*, won prizes when it was first shown in 2006. And the story continues …

*Captain Jack Sparrow*

## Chapter 1  Jack Sparrow's Return

The moon was high above a dark ocean. A stone prison stood above a beach. A group of guards carried six wooden boxes to the prison wall and threw them into the ocean below.

Suddenly, there was a gunshot inside one of the boxes. An arm reached through the newly made hole and opened the box. It was Captain Jack Sparrow, the smartest pirate who ever sailed the ocean.

As he looked around, his gold tooth shone in the moonlight.

Jack seemed calm … at first. Then his eyes grew round with fear and he quickly searched the box. He found it—his hat! He placed the hat on his head and smiled.

He reached into the box again. "Sorry, my friend," he said. He pulled hard at the leg bone of the other body in the box.

With the bone in his hands, he lowered one end into the water. Then he rowed the box toward his ship, the *Black Pearl*.

Gibbs, a fine old pirate, was waiting on the *Pearl* for Jack's return. He helped his captain onto the ship.

Jack took a piece of cloth from his jacket and looked at it carefully.

"So you found something?" asked a toothless pirate named Leech. Every man on the ship wanted news about the treasure.

"Yes, but I haven't studied it yet," Jack said.

Suddenly, a small monkey jumped in front of Jack and screamed. It took the piece of cloth and ran into the sails. When the moon shone on the monkey, its skin disappeared. Only its bones were left. This was Captain Barbossa's monkey and, like its owner, it was cursed. It was the living dead.

Jack hated the animal. He took out his gun and shot at it. The monkey fell and dropped the cloth, but quickly jumped up again. It smiled.

One of the pirates caught the piece of cloth.

"It's a key," he said.

"It's even better than a key," Jack said. "It's a *drawing* of a key."

The sailors didn't understand. They looked at Gibbs.

"Captain," Gibbs said. "We wanted gold, and …"

Jack turned to his men. "What do keys do?" he asked.

"They unlock things," Leech said, suddenly excited.

"Important things," Gibbs said. He imagined chests full of gold. "So we're going to unlock something!"

Jack shook his head. "No. We don't have the key yet, so we can't unlock anything, stupid!"

The sailors looked at Jack. "So we're going to find the key?" Gibbs asked.

"A key won't help us," Jack said impatiently. "We don't know what it opens. Please," he added, "try to understand!"

"So which way are we going?" another pirate asked.

"Ah, yes …" Jack opened his Compass. On his last adventure, this Compass took him to *Isla de Muerta* and the hidden treasure. But this time he seemed unhappy when he looked at it.

He closed it quickly and waved his arm. "Pull up the sails. Let's go … that way," he finally said, pointing toward the ocean.

"Captain?" Gibbs asked.

"I'll plan our trip later. Now hurry and start sailing!" Jack ordered.

The men were unhappy, but prepared to sail.

"The captain's acting a little … strange," one pirate said quietly to Gibbs.

"Yes," Gibbs answered. "He doesn't know where we're going!"

♦

Outside a small church in the Caribbean town of Port Royal, Elizabeth Swann was on her knees in her wedding dress. Her tears mixed with the rain. Around her were overturned chairs … and no husband. Slowly, she went inside to wait.

Through her tears she saw a man come into the church. With him were an officer and a group of soldiers who were pushing a prisoner. The prisoner was the man she wanted to marry, Will Turner.

"Will!" Elizabeth called. "What's happening?"

"I don't know," Will said sadly. "You look beautiful," he added softly.

"You! Free the prisoner immediately," said a loud voice from the door. It was Elizabeth's father, Governor Swann. He looked angrily at the officer.

The officer didn't move. Governor Swann studied the man's face.

"Cutler Beckett?" he asked finally.

"It's *Lord* Beckett now," the man replied.

"Lord or not, do you have a reason to arrest this man?"

"I do. Mr. Mercer?" Beckett said to a man next to him.

Mercer gave him a letter. Governor Swann looked at it.

"This letter isn't for the arrest of Will Turner!" he said. "This is for the arrest of Elizabeth Swann!"

"Is it?" Beckett asked. "My mistake. Arrest her," he ordered.

The soldiers took Elizabeth.

"Why?" Elizabeth asked angrily.

Beckett didn't answer. He produced two more letters.

"Here's the letter for William Turner. And this one orders the arrest of James Norrington. Do you know where he is?"

"Commodore Norrington left here some months ago," the governor answered quickly. "We don't know where he is."

"Why are you arresting us?" Elizabeth asked bravely.

Beckett looked at his prisoners. "You helped a pirate to escape. The punishment for that is death," he said happily. "You remember Jack Sparrow, don't you?"

Will looked at Elizabeth. "*Captain* Jack Sparrow," they said together.

"Yes," Beckett answered. He turned to his men. "Take them away."

◆

Captain Jack Sparrow had his own problems. Alone in his room on the *Black Pearl*, he held his Compass tightly in his hand. He looked at it and quickly closed it. Then he shook it and looked at it again. Not good. He reached for a drink. The bottle was empty. He left the room to find another bottle.

The drinks cupboard was almost empty. He smiled when he saw a bottle on the lower shelf. He opened it and turned it over. Sand fell onto the floor.

"You have no more time, Jack," a voice said suddenly.

Jack turned. In front of him was a man's face, covered with animals and plants from the bottom of the ocean.

"Bootstrap?" Jack asked. "Bill Turner?"

"Yes, Jack Sparrow. You look good."

Jack looked at the sailor. "You don't," he said. "Is this a dream?"

"No." Bootstrap said. He gave Jack a drink. "You got the *Pearl* back," he said.

"Your son helped me," Jack told him.

Now Bootstrap was surprised. "William? A pirate?"

"Yes," Jack said. "He's too honest, though," he added. "So why are you here?"

"Davy Jones sent me," Bootstrap answered. "I'm sorry that I fought against you. Everything went wrong after we took your ship. I was cursed, and at the bottom of the ocean. I couldn't move and I couldn't die." Jack looked afraid. "Then Davy Jones came to me and made an offer. If I spend one hundred years on his ship, I can rest after that."

Bootstrap looked at his old captain. "He wants you. He owns you, too, Jack. He lifted the *Pearl* from the ocean floor for you. You were her captain for thirteen years."

Jack started to speak, but Bootstrap stopped him. "You can't stop the curse," he said. "Your soul will spend a lifetime on his ship."

"Davy's ship, the *Flying Dutchman*, already has a captain," Jack said quickly. "He doesn't need me."

Bootstrap shook his head sadly. Captain Jack Sparrow never stopped fighting.

"It's Davy Jones's world for you, Jack. Jones will send his monster, the Kraken, and pull the *Pearl* back down to the bottom of the ocean … and you with it."

"Any idea when?" Jack asked. He tried not to sound worried.

Bootstrap lifted his arm and pointed to Jack's hand. Jack stepped away, but it was too late. There was a black mark on his hand. He was now a marked man!

"He'll find you," Bootstrap said.

Jack looked up, but Bootstrap Bill was gone. Jack screamed and ran through the ship.

"Get up!" he shouted to his sleeping men. "Hurry!"

Then he tied a cloth around his hand, covering the black mark. He didn't want anyone to see it.

Gibbs found Jack behind the mast. "Where are we going?" he asked.

"We're going to land!" Jack shouted.

"Which port?" Gibbs asked.

"Land! It doesn't matter where."

The monkey jumped down from the mast onto Jack's shoulder and knocked his hat into the ocean.

"Jack's hat!" Gibbs cried to the other men. He knew the captain loved his hat. "Turn the ship around!"

"No!" Jack said quickly. "Leave it."

His men were surprised.

Gibbs turned to Jack. "What's coming after us?" he asked quietly.

♦

Captain Jack Sparrow's hat sailed far away from the *Black Pearl*. A sailor on a fishing boat picked it up. He liked it and put it on his head. When another sailor tried to take it from him, the two men began to fight.

Suddenly, the boat shook. The sailors looked around, then down at the hat. They tried to throw it into the ocean. Too late! Their boat broke into pieces and was pulled down into the ocean …

Then the water was calm again.

## Chapter 2  The Search for the *Black Pearl*

Two guards took Will Turner into Lord Beckett's office.

"Are you going to free Elizabeth?" Will asked.

"If you help me, I'll free her," Beckett answered. "We want you to find Captain Sparrow. I want you to get something that belongs to him."

"You want the *Black Pearl*?" Will said.

Beckett was surprised. "The *Black Pearl*? No, I want something that's smaller and much more important. Something that Sparrow carries at all times. A compass. Bring back the Compass—then I will free Elizabeth."

Will Turner angrily left Beckett's office and went to Elizabeth's room in the prison building. Governor Swann followed him and heard them talking.

"Jack's Compass? Why does Beckett want that?"

"His reason isn't important," Will said. "I'll find Jack and bring him back to Port Royal. Then we'll both be free."

"How are you going to find him?" Elizabeth asked, worried. Her voice showed her fear.

"Tortuga. I'll start there. I won't stop until I find him. Then I'll return and marry you."

♦

Will Turner started his search immediately. He went to Tortuga because Jack often stayed there. It was the dirtiest port in the Caribbean, a place for drunken pirates who wanted adventures.

When he arrived, Will saw a friend of Jack's; a woman with red hair and a red dress. Her name was Scarlett.

"I haven't seen him for a month," Scarlett said angrily. "When you find him, give him a message."

She lifted her hand and hit Will across the face.

"I don't know about Jack, but there's a ship with black sails at an island south of here," said an old boatman. "Give me some money and I'll take you to it."

The boatman took Will to the island and there they found the *Black Pearl* on its side on the beach. The boatman refused to go closer, so Will jumped into the water. He swam to the beach and then, very wet, walked across to the ship.

There was nobody there, but he found an old fire in the sand. The firewood was still warm. Jack was near!

"Jack!" Will shouted. "Jack Sparrow! Mr. Gibbs! …"

He pulled out his sword and went into the forest. There, he noticed a small red bottle on the ground.

"Gibbs …" Will thought. "That's his bottle!"

He picked it up. A fishing line was tied to the bottle and Will put his hand on it. Then, suddenly, he noticed two eyes in a tree— and an arm that pulled the line hard!

Will was pulled off his feet. As he hung by his leg from a tree, he saw a group of islanders. They had bite marks on their faces and bodies and they were wearing bones around their necks.

The islanders ran toward Will and he kicked some of them to the ground with his free leg.

"Come here and fight!" he shouted at one of the men.

The man quickly shot a drug into Will's neck. Will stopped moving and the men cut him down from the tree.

♦

In her small room in Port Royal prison, Elizabeth waited. She was tired and closed her eyes. Then she heard the sound of keys and a guard opened the door.

"Come quickly!" her father said, stepping out of the shadows behind the guard.

"What's happening?" Elizabeth asked.

"You can return to England," Governor Swann said. "I've found a ship for you. Hawkins, the captain, is an old friend of mine."

They ran quickly out of the prison.

The governor took Elizabeth to a waiting vehicle pulled by two horses, but she refused to get in.

"I'm waiting for Will," she said.

"We can't wait for Will's help," the governor said. "I'm not going to watch my daughter die."

He pushed her inside and put a gun in her hand. Then he shut the door and quickly drove the vehicle to the ship.

Near the port, the governor slowed the horses. Two men were waiting in the shadows. One of them wore a captain's hat.

The governor jumped down from his seat and hurried to the men.

"Captain Hawkins!" he said, happy to see his friend.

But Hawkins didn't answer.

The captain fell to the ground, covered in blood. The governor realized that the other man in the shadows was holding up the captain's dead body.

"Good evening, Governor," the second man said, slowly

cleaning blood from his knife with a cloth. Swann knew the man: Mercer, Beckett's assistant.

Governor Swann ran back to the vehicle.

"Elizabeth," he shouted.

Mercer called some soldiers. He smiled as he opened the vehicle door.

It was empty!

"Where is she?" Mercer said angrily.

"Who?" Swann asked nervously.

Mercer pushed the governor against the vehicle and shouted, "Elizabeth!"

"She never listened to me," the governor said, and smiled.

"Take him away!" Mercer ordered the soldiers.

♦

Lord Beckett walked into his dark office and stopped.

"There's somebody here," he thought.

Elizabeth stepped out of the shadows and lifted her father's gun.

"I have information," she said. "You sent Will to find Jack Sparrow's Compass. But it won't help you. I saw the treasure on *Isla de Muerta* and you need to know something."

Beckett smiled. "You think that the Compass only points to *Isla de Muerta*. You're wrong, Miss Swann. The cursed gold is not important." He pointed to a big world map. "There is more than one treasure chest in these oceans," he said.

Elizabeth pointed the gun at Lord Beckett's head.

"These letters on your desk will free Will Turner," she said. "Sign them."

Beckett stopped laughing and signed the letters.

"I want the Compass," he said.

Elizabeth took the letters, turned, and disappeared silently into the dark night.

The following morning, the *Edinburgh Trader* sailed from Port Royal. One of the sailors was Elizabeth. She was dressed in sailor's clothes, and none of the men on the ship noticed her.

## Chapter 3  The Island of the Pelegostos

When Will Turner woke up, his hands and feet were tied. The islanders were carrying him toward some wooden houses. Finally, they put him down in front of a large chair.

He looked up … and smiled. A man was sitting on the chair, and it was Captain Jack Sparrow!

*A man was sitting on the chair, and it was Captain Jack Sparrow!*

"Jack Sparrow," Will said, "I am very happy to see you."

Jack didn't answer.

"Jack? Jack, it's me, Will Turner. Tell them to free me."

Jack stepped down from his chair and spoke in a strange language. Will suddenly noticed the dead men's bones around the chair.

"Jack, listen," Will said. "I need the Compass. Elizabeth is in danger. We were arrested for helping you. She's going to die!"

One of the islanders pointed at Will's leg and hungrily touched his stomach. Jack smiled and the men shouted happily.

"No!" Will screamed. "Jack, what did you say to them?"

But Jack didn't answer. He climbed back on to his chair and looked over Will's head.

The men started to pull Will away.

"They're going to prepare me for dinner," he thought.

Jack suddenly looked down at Will. "Save me!" the captain said quietly out of the corner of his mouth.

The men threw Will into a cage full of men, chained to a rocky hill. Some of the sailors from the *Black Pearl* were prisoners in another cage.

"Will, you shouldn't be here!" Gibbs greeted him.

"Why is this happening?" Will asked. He looked at the sailors. "Jack seems to be the chief …"

"Yes," Gibbs said sadly. "The Pelegostos made him their chief. And now they want to free his soul from his body. They're going to cook him and eat him."

"Where are the other sailors from the *Pearl*?" Will asked.

"Look more carefully at these cages," Gibbs said quietly. "The Pelegostos built them after we arrived."

Will looked at the walls of his cage. They were made of bones. He quickly moved his hand away.

"The meal starts when the sun goes down," Gibbs said seriously. "Jack's life will end when the music stops."

♦

In a small boat near the beach, two of Barbossa's pirates, Pintel and Ragetti, rowed with their backs to the sun. A dog with a ring of keys in its mouth was sitting at the end of the boat.

Suddenly, the men saw the *Black Pearl*.

"Look! There it is!" Pintel cried.

The dog jumped into the clear blue water and swam to the beach.

Pintel looked up at the ship's black sails. "It's ours!" he said greedily.

Then they heard the sound of music through the trees.

♦

The music on the island grew louder as the Pelegostos prepared their big meal. Captain Jack Sparrow was their special guest—and their main course. He tried to smile.

The islanders placed a long, thin piece of wood above an unlit fire. Jack looked at it and turned away.

"We need a bigger fire!" he shouted in the language of the Pelegostos. "*I am the chief. I need more wood! Big fire!* MORE WOOD!"

The islanders hurried away in search of more wood. Jack waited until every man was gone. Then he ran and ran.

When he arrived at a small house, a large man opened the door.

Jack stepped back.

"I'm not running away—nooo …," he said.

Soon he was tied to the long piece of wood over the unlit fire. The fire was now very big.

"Nice work," he said. The Pelegostos smiled proudly. "Too nice," Jack thought to himself.

♦

On the rocky hill, Will and the pirates waited in their bone cages.

"I must do something," Will said to himself. "I must save Elizabeth."

"Try to move your cage!" he shouted to the pirates. "Move it toward the rocks! Then put your feet through the holes between the bones and try to climb the hill."

Leech and the pirates in the other cage understood and started to move it slowly up the hill. But suddenly, a guard saw them and screamed loudly. The music stopped.

As Will and the men in his cage reached the top of the hill, the islanders ran toward them. They pulled the cage up around their legs and started to run. They had to find the *Black Pearl*. Fast!

When the guard ran toward them, the Pelegostos were preparing to light the fire under Jack.

"The prisoners are trying to escape!" he screamed.

"*Follow them!*" Jack ordered. "*They mustn't escape!*"

"What shall we do?" The Pelegostos islanders couldn't decide. "Shall we light the fire or follow the other prisoners? We want to free our chief from his body, but he is telling us to leave."

Finally, they decided to follow the other prisoners. But one man dropped a piece of burning wood, and suddenly the fire was burning under Jack. There was nothing that Jack could do about it.

"They're going to cook me—Captain Jack Sparrow!" he said to himself.

Jack finally escaped from the burning wood by throwing his body from one side to the other. Watched by a small boy, he jumped away from the fire and ran into the trees.

The boy also ran into the forest and found the Pelegostos.

"Our chief is running away!" he called.

The islanders shouted angrily. They stopped following Jack's men and ran after Jack.

Will and some of the pirates arrived on the beach and broke out of their cage. They didn't notice Pintel and Ragetti preparing the *Pearl*.

"Excellent!" Gibbs shouted. "We can sail."

"I'm not going to leave without Jack," Will said.

Gibbs suddenly pointed along the beach and Will saw Jack. He was running down the beach with the Pelegostos close behind him.

"Jack! Hurry!" Gibbs shouted.

Jack ran through the shallow water to the side of the *Pearl*, and Gibbs pulled him onto the ship.

## Chapter 4  The Secret of the Dead Man's Chest

Jack Sparrow sat at the front of the *Black Pearl*.

"Do you want us to sail away from the island?" Gibbs asked him.

"Yes, but stay in shallow water," Jack replied.

He opened his Compass and looked at it carefully. Will Turner stood next to him.

"Jack," he said quietly.

"Not now," Jack answered, with his eyes still on the Compass.

"Jack, I need …"

"Not *now*," Jack said angrily, reaching for his gun. Finally, he saw Will. "Oh. It's you."

"Jack," Will said again. "I need that Compass."

"Why?" Jack asked. He looked at the Compass again, then closed it.

"I want to save Elizabeth," Will said.

Jack shook his head. "I've heard those words before," he said. "We saved *Elizabeth* before. Why don't you watch her more carefully? Lock her up in a room?"

"She *is* locked up. In prison. She's going to die because she helped you."

Jack started to climb up into the sails.

"That isn't my problem," he said.

Suddenly, he felt the cold touch of Will's sword at his neck.

"Give me the Compass. Now! Then the English will stop looking for you."

Jack said slowly, "All right. You get the Compass and you save your pretty girl. What do *I* get?"

"You'll be free. The English will stop searching for you," Will explained again.

"I will give you the Compass," Jack said slowly. "But you must find something for me. It's quite dangerous …"

He pulled the small piece of cloth out of his pocket. Will looked at the picture of the key on the cloth.

"Is this going to save Elizabeth?" he asked.

Jack put his mouth close to Will's ear. "How much do you know about Davy Jones?" he said very quietly.

"Nothing," Will said.

Jack smiled. "Yes," he said. "It's going to save Elizabeth."

♦

On the *Edinburgh Trader* Elizabeth Swann, dressed in a sailor's clothes, was on her way to Tortuga. She was hoping to find Will. But Will was nowhere near Tortuga now. He, Jack Sparrow, and Jack's men were traveling down the Pantano River in two rowing boats.

"Why is Jack so nervous?" Will asked Gibbs quietly.

"He's made an enemy of Davy Jones," Gibbs said seriously. "He thinks that he's only safe on land. If he goes out onto the ocean, Davy Jones will take him."

"Davy Jones?"

"Well, he has a monster that works for him. The Kraken,"

Gibbs said. His voice shook. "It's terrible—it can pull a ship to the bottom of the ocean …"

Gibbs stopped, and Will saw the fear in his eyes.

"Is Jack afraid to die?" asked Will.

"Davy Jones doesn't kill you," Gibbs answered. "He punishes you. Think of the worst thing in the world. It's waiting for you in Davy Jones's world. And it never ends."

"And the key will save him?" Will asked finally.

"That's the question that Jack wants to answer. So he's going to visit … her."

"Her?" Will asked nervously.

"Yes—her."

The rowing boats stopped near a small wooden house high in a tree. There was a light outside the door.

"Don't worry," Jack called to the other men. He tried to speak happily. "Tia Dalma and I are old friends."

"I'll watch your back," Gibbs offered.

"I'm more worried about my front," Jack said quietly.

As Jack climbed up into the house, the other pirates stayed close behind him. In the low light, they saw many strange animals in glass bottles. Ragetti touched his wooden eye when he noticed a bottle of eyes in a corner.

Tia Dalma sat at a table in the shadows. She wasn't surprised by the visitors because she could see into the future. She stood.

"Jack Sparrow," she said, "I knew the wind would bring you back to me one day."

Her eyes moved past Jack to Will. She smiled as she looked at him.

"I can see a great future for you, William Turner," she said, moving closer.

"Do you know me?" Will asked.

"*You* want to know *me*," she replied.

She looked into his eyes and pulled him close.

*She looked into his eyes...*

Jack walked to Tia Dalma and pushed her back toward the table.

"We need your help," he said.

"Is Jack Sparrow asking for help?" she asked, amused.

"It's not for me," Jack answered. "It's for William. If you help me, I will help him."

Tia Dalma smiled. "How can I help you? How will you pay me?"

"I will pay you with this!" Jack said brightly.

He took a wooden box from Pintel's hand. Inside was the monkey. Jack lifted his gun and shot it. The little monkey looked angrily at him.

"The pay is fair," Tia Dalma agreed. Her eyes moved again to Will.

Jack passed the picture of the key to Will, and he quickly showed it to Tia Dalma.

"We're looking for this. What does it unlock?" Will asked.

Tia Dalma spoke to Jack. "Your key opens a chest …"

"What is inside the chest?" Gibbs asked.

"Gold? Treasure?" Pintel said, his voice full of hope.

"Nothing bad, I hope," Ragetti said nervously.

Tia Dalma smiled at the pirates. Then she told her story.

"You know about Davy Jones? A man of the ocean, a great sailor until he met man's biggest problem."

"What is man's biggest problem?" Will asked her.

"The ocean," Gibbs said seriously.

Tia Dalma shook her head.

"Adding numbers," Pintel said.

Tia Dalma shook her head again.

"The difference between good and bad," Ragetti suggested.

Everyone in the room looked at the one-eyed pirate and shook their heads.

"A woman," Jack said, ending the game.

Tia Dalma smiled at the rough pirate. "A woman. He fell in love, but his love brought great pain. He couldn't live with the pain—but he couldn't die."

The pirates smiled sadly. They understood the story.

"Exactly *what* did he put into the chest?" Will asked.

"He cut his heart out of his body and put it in a chest. He hid the chest from the world …. He keeps the key with him at all times."

Will finally understood. The key opened the chest that held Jones's heart.

"You knew this," Will said to Jack.

"No, I didn't …" Jack said nervously. "Well, I didn't know

where the key was."

Will didn't believe him.

"But now we know," Jack said smoothly. "You can go onto Jones's ship, the *Flying Dutchman*, and take the key. Then you can go back to Port Royal and save your pretty girlfriend."

Jack moved toward the door. Tia Dalma spoke before he opened it.

"Show me your hand," she said.

Slowly, Jack untied the cloth. Tia Dalma looked carefully at the black mark.

Gibbs saw the mark, too. Pintel and Ragetti watched the old pirate turn in a circle three times for good luck. Not knowing why, they also turned three times.

Tia Dalma moved across the room and climbed the stairs. At the top, she opened a great door. The sound of the ocean came quietly from outside it. Tia Dalma slowly closed the door and came down the stairs again. In her hands she carried a large bottle with a wide top that she gave to Jack.

"Davy Jones can step on land only once every ten years," she said to him. She put some earth into the bottle. "You are safe on land, Jack Sparrow, so carry the land with you."

Jack looked into the bottle. "Is this bottle of earth really going to help me?" he asked.

Tia Dalma reached out her hand for the bottle.

"If you don't want it, give it back to me."

"No!" Jack cried, and held the bottle to his chest.

"Then it will help you," she said.

Will looked at Tia Dalma. "We need to find Davy Jones and the *Flying Dutchman*," he said.

Tia Dalma smiled at his young face, then sat at her table again.

"I'll tell you where to go," she said.

## Chapter 5  Will Meets Davy Jones

The pirates left Tia Dalma's house and sailed the *Black Pearl* to an island. They came to a ship that lay on its side in shallow water.

Jack and Gibbs stood under an oil light and looked silently at the old, broken ship.

"Is that the *Flying Dutchman*?" Will asked. "She doesn't look very good."

"What's your plan?" Jack asked.

"I'll search the ship until I find your key," Will said.

"And if you find sailors on the ship?" Jack asked him.

"I'll kill them."

Jack smiled. "I like your plan. It's simple and easy to remember."

"I'll bring you the key, and you'll give me the Compass," Will said.

"Yes," Jack agreed. "If anyone catches you, use these words: 'Jack Sparrow sent me. He wants me to pay you.'" Then he added, "It will save your life."

Will said goodbye and climbed into a rowing boat. Jack watched silently. Then he ordered Gibbs to turn out the *Black Pearl*'s lights. Soon only Captain Jack Sparrow's gold-toothed smile shone in the dark.

Will reached the broken old ship and lit a small oil light. Was the ship empty? He saw the bodies of many dead seamen and felt very nervous.

"What happened here?" he asked himself.

Suddenly, he heard a noise. Will turned and saw a sailor. He was badly hurt but he was trying to pull up a sail.

"Sailor, it's no good," Will said. "The water is too shallow. Your ship won't move."

But the man kept trying. "No … below us … the ocean took Billy and Quentin … captain's orders!"

The ship shook and a dead sailor dropped from the mast. Will saw round, red marks on the man's back. He turned the body over. The man's face was gone!

"Something has eaten him!" Will thought. The Kraken! He remembered Gibbs's description of the monster.

Will moved away from the body. Suddenly, the ocean was very calm. Then, very quickly, the wind came and the water turned white and stormy. Will saw a great ship come up from the bottom of the ocean. It was the *Flying Dutchman*!

"Jack tricked me!" Will thought. "He sent me to this old ship. He knew that Davy Jones would follow me."

The real *Flying Dutchman* was made of pale wood and bones. Animals and plants from the ocean floor covered every inch of it.

The *Dutchman*'s sailors climbed onto the old ship. Will pulled out his sword and ran toward his rowing boat. Maccus, one of the *Dutchman*'s sailors, stopped him. The other sailors joined Maccus and stood around Will.

"Get down on your knees!" Greenbeard, another sailor, said angrily.

Will quickly pushed his sword into his oil light. Burning oil covered the sword, and Will attacked the sailors. He fought hard, but suddenly something hit him in the face. As he fell, the *Dutchman*'s sailors moved toward him …

When he woke up, Will was still on the old ship. He was at the end of a line of sailors, all on their knees. Someone walked slowly toward them. It was Davy Jones!

Jones was very ugly, with blue eyes and a long beard. His left hand and one of his legs were missing. He looked angrily down at the line of sailors in front of him.

"Six men are still alive," Maccus said.

Jones walked down the line. "Do you fear death?" he asked a sailor. "I can offer you—an escape."

"Don't listen to him!" said another man in the line. He held a cross in his hand.

Jones turned and shouted at the second man, "Don't you fear death?"

"No, sir."

"Good luck, friend," Jones said.

He smiled, then turned to Greenbeard. Greenbeard threw the man into the ocean.

Jones moved close to the first sailor. "Life is painful but you fear death. You can join my ship and escape it. You must spend one hundred years on the *Flying Dutchman*. Will you come with me?"

The sailor said quickly, "I will come with you."

Jones smiled and moved down the line. He stopped next to Will.

"You are neither dead nor dying. Why are you here?"

"Jack Sparrow sent me," Will replied. "He wants me to pay you."

Jones looked very angry. "Does he? Shall I accept that offer?"

He turned his head and looked out across the dark ocean.

Hiding in darkness on the *Black Pearl*, Jack Sparrow watched the *Flying Dutchman*. Jones was looking straight at him! Then, Davy Jones suddenly arrived in front of him. The *Dutchman's* sailors also flew onto the *Pearl*, and quickly circled round Jack and his pirates.

"It's time to pay me," Jones said to Jack. His voice was low and angry. "I made you captain of the *Black Pearl* for thirteen years. Now I want your soul."

"Well," Jack said, "I was only captain for two years—then my men stole the ship."

"But you *were* a captain," Jones replied. "You introduce yourself as Captain Jack Sparrow."

"I've already paid you. I've sent you a soul to work on your ship. He's over there," Jack said. He was talking about Will.

"You can't send another soul," Jones shouted. "One soul is not the same as another!"

"So how many souls do you want for mine?" Jack asked.

Jones thought about Jack's question. Finally he said, "One hundred souls. In three days."

Jack gave Jones a big smile. "Thanks, friend. Send the boy back to me. I'll start looking for those souls."

"I'll keep the boy. You must find ninety-nine more."

"Ninety-nine?" Jack asked, seeming surprised. "Have you met Will Turner? He's a good and brave man. His soul is as good as four ordinary souls …"

"I'll keep the boy!" Jones repeated. "Bring me ninety-nine more souls. In three days. Do you accept this offer?"

Jack thought about the question.

"Yes," he answered.

"This Will Turner is a good man and he's your friend. Do you want him to stay with me for the rest of his life?" Jones asked.

"Yes, that's OK," Jack answered, and smiled.

He looked down at his hand. The black mark was gone. When he looked up, Davy Jones and his sailors were gone, too.

Minutes later, the *Flying Dutchman* and Will sailed away into a storm. Jack watched silently as the ship disappeared.

"I have three days to find ninety-nine souls. There's only one place to go—Tortuga," he thought.


## Chapter 6  Captain Sparrow Sails Again

Jack sat in a corner of a crowded bar in Tortuga. His feet were on a table and his Compass was in his hand.

Gibbs was finding Jack's ninety-nine souls. He promised an exciting life on the *Black Pearl* to a line of hopeful sailors. Because they were in Tortuga, every man was old and sick.

"I have one arm and a bad leg," an old sailor told Gibbs.

"We can use you," Gibbs replied.

After a few more interviews, he walked over to Jack.

"How many?" Jack asked, looking up.

"With those four?" Gibbs said unhappily. "We have four." Gibbs was worried. "I don't want anything to happen to *me*," he added quickly.

"I'm not making any promises," Jack said. He didn't like promises.

"Make a new plan, Jack. And don't use that Compass. We all know that it hasn't worked for a long time."

Jack looked angrily at Gibbs.

"What's your story?" Gibbs asked the next sailor. The man was drunk and unshaven, but his eyes were clear.

"My story?" the man replied. "It's the same as your story. I wanted to catch a well-known pirate. I followed him across the seven oceans. I lost my ship, my job, my life."

Gibbs looked more closely at the man. "Commodore?" he asked. Was this really Commodore Norrington, the man who followed Jack and the *Pearl* to *Isla de Muerta*?

"I'm not a commodore now," Norrington answered. He threw his bottle down onto the table. "So, can I join your ship?"

Gibbs was too surprised to answer. The silence made Norrington angry.

"So, can I work for Captain Jack Sparrow?" he shouted. Then he turned to Jack and pulled out his gun. "Or shall I kill you now?"

On his way out of the door, Jack stopped and smiled quickly.

"You can join us, friend!"

Norrington didn't put his gun down.

"Sorry," he said. "But I really want to shoot you …"

"Calm down, soldier," a man said, and held Norrington's arm. "That's our captain."

Norrington's gunshot just missed the man. Jack's new sailors jumped up and started to fight. Other pirates joined the fight. Chairs fell to the floor and bottles were broken.

"We'll leave now," Jack said quietly to Gibbs.

He walked carefully through the fight, unhurt. He picked up a hat from the floor and put it on his head. It was too small.

"It's hard to find a good hat these days," he said to himself.

He and Gibbs walked quietly away.

Norrington had a sword in his hand now. "Fight, then. You, you, you!" he shouted drunkenly. Then someone hit him over the head with a bottle and he fell to the floor.

Elizabeth stood over him, dressed in her sailor's clothes.

"I just wanted to hit him," she shouted to the pirates. "Now throw him out of the bar and we'll have a drink!" Then, as the pirates shouted their agreement, she looked carefully at the man on the floor. "I don't believe it!" she said quietly. "James Norrington. What has the world done to you?"

She helped him to his feet and they walked slowly toward the port. Suddenly, they were standing in front of Jack.

"Captain Sparrow," Elizabeth said to him.

Jack looked at her, but didn't know her in her sailor's clothes.

"Do you want to join my ship, boy?" he said. "Welcome!"

"I want to find the man I love," Elizabeth replied. "William Turner."

"Elizabeth?" Jack said, looking at her carefully. "You don't look good in those clothes, you know."

"Jack," Elizabeth said, "I know that Will followed you. Where is he?"

"I'm really sorry, but Will has joined Davy Jones's ship."

"Davy Jones," Elizabeth repeated.

"Oh, please," Norrington laughed. "The captain of the *Flying Dutchman*? A ship that takes dead men from this world to the next … ?"

"Correct!" Jack said. He looked closely at Norrington. "I know you! Commodore! You look terrible, friend. Why are you here?"

"I joined your ship," Norrington replied.

"Jack," Elizabeth said, "I want to find Will."

Jack pulled his black beard. "Are you sure?" he asked. "Is that what you really want?"

"Of course," Elizabeth answered. "Do you know how I can save him?"

"Well," Jack began slowly, "there is a chest. A chest of unknown size. Jones will do anything to keep that chest. The chest can save Will."

"How can we find it?" Elizabeth asked.

Jack placed the Compass in her hand. "With this. This Compass will point to the thing that you want most in this world."

"Jack, is the story about the chest true?" Elizabeth asked.

"Every word is true, love. You want to find Davy Jones's chest, don't you?"

"I want to save Will," Elizabeth agreed.

Jack opened the Compass in her hand and looked at it. He turned to Gibbs.

"We go that way!" he shouted, and pointed toward the ocean.


## Chapter 7  A Very Important Game

Davy Jones sat on the *Flying Dutchman*. He was playing slow, sad music on a piano. His eyes filled with tears as he looked up at a picture of a woman with long, thick hair.

The sailors—and Will Turner—were working hard. Will was pulling a chain when suddenly he dropped it.

"Careless!" one of the sailors shouted. "I'll punish you for that mistake."

He started to hit Will, but Bootstrap Bill stopped him.

"I'll punish you, too," the sailor told him angrily.

"That's all right," Bootstrap told him. "You can punish me."

"Why?" Davy Jones asked. He stopped playing the piano and watched the men carefully.

Bootstrap lifted his hand and pointed at Will. "My son. That's my son."

Will's eyes widened. The old pirate was his father?

Jones smiled. "This is very interesting," he said. "Do you want to stop this sailor punishing your son?"

"Yes," Bootstrap answered.

"Then you can punish him yourself! Hit him!"

"I can't hit my own son!" Bootstrap Bill said.

"Then another sailor will punish him."

"No," Bootstrap shouted quickly. He lifted his arm and started to hit Will.

Later, Bootstrap explained his actions to his son. "That sailor is a hard man. I didn't want him to hurt you."

"So you saved me," Will said, thoughtfully.

Bootstrap shook his head sadly. "I can't save you from the *Dutchman*," he said. "You made a promise to Davy Jones. Now you can't leave his ship. Your body will become part of it. Look at old Wyvern."

Bootstrap pointed at the side of the ship. An old man hung there. He seemed to be part of the ship.

"But I didn't make any promises to Davy Jones," Will said.

Bootstrap looked happier. "Then you must escape."

"Not until I find this key," Will said, He showed his father the picture of the key. "It's on the ship and Jack Sparrow wants it. Maybe it will save us."

Suddenly, old Wyvern moved and pulled himself free from the side of the ship.

"The Dead Man's Chest!" he cried.

His arms reached for the cloth.

Will jumped back, afraid. "This is what happens to Davy Jones's men," he said to himself. "Soon my father will become part of the *Dutchman*, too—just one more unhappy soul."

But Wyvern's next words made Will more hopeful.

"Open the chest with the key, and cut through the heart with your sword," old Wyvern cried. Then he changed his mind. "Don't destroy the heart! The *Dutchman* must have a living heart or there is no captain! And if there is no captain, no one will hold the key!"

"The captain has the key?" Will asked.

"Hidden," Wyvern said. He disappeared again into the side of the ship.

But Will had his answer. Jones had the key.

♦

On the *Black Pearl*, Jack Sparrow found Elizabeth filling in names on Lord Beckett's letters. These letters would free Jack from the English.

Jack immediately took them from her. "These letters belong to *me*, don't they?" He looked at the signature on the papers. "Lord Cutler Beckett. Is *he* the man who wants my Compass?"

"Not the Compass—a chest," Elizabeth said.

Gibbs heard her words and looked up. "A chest? Not Davy Jones's chest? If Beckett has the chest, the oceans will be his."

"So that's why Beckett wants it," Elizabeth thought.

Jack looked carefully at the letters. "Beckett will free me and I can work for the English." He laughed. "I can't think of anything worse."

He shook his head and put the letters in his jacket pocket.

"Jack," Elizabeth said. "Give the letters back to me."

Jack looked at her. "Take them from me," he said, smiling.

Elizabeth turned away from the pirate.

Norrington was standing near them, listening. As Elizabeth passed, he stopped her.

"Ask yourself a question," he said. "Who sent Will onto the *Flying Dutchman*?"

♦

On the *Dutchman*, some of the sailors were playing a numbers game. Will watched the game and tried to understand it.

"What are they playing for?" Will asked Bootstrap. The old sailor was standing behind his son.

"The only thing any of us can offer," Bootstrap told him. "Years of service on this ship."

"Can anyone play?" Will asked his father slowly.

"Yes," Bootstrap replied.

"Then I want to play with Davy Jones," Will said loudly.

The sailors went silent. Suddenly, Jones stood in front of them.

"I accept," he told Will. "But I'll only play for the thing that is most important to a man's heart."

"I'll offer one hundred years of service on your ship," was Will's reply.

*"I'll offer one hundred years of service on your ship."*

"No!" Bootstrap cried.

"And I'll free you, if you win," Jones said.

"I'm already free," Will thought. He didn't know about Jack's trick.

"No, I want you to free my father," he said.

"I agree," Jones answered. He sat down opposite Will. "You're a crazy young man," Jones said. "You want to get married and you will get married—to this ship."

They began to play. Will won the first game. His father was free, but Will wanted more.

"Another game," he said suddenly, to the surprise of the sailors.

"You can't win again, son," Jones said, and stood up.

Will smiled. "Then why are you walking away?" he asked.

Jones looked very angry. "What will you play for?" he asked, and sat down again.

"My soul," Will answered. "If I lose, I'll work for you until the end of time."

"And if you win?" Jones asked.

"I want the thing that is dearest to *your* heart," Will said. "I want this." He showed Jones the cloth with the picture of the key.

Jones lifted his head. "How do you know about the key?" he asked sharply.

"I don't have to tell you. That's not part of the game, is it?" Will asked.

Jones reached into his shirt and pulled out the key. It hung on a chain around his neck.

"Now I know where it's hidden," Will thought.

Bootstrap stepped between them. "I want to play," he said. "If I lose, you can have my soul too. If I win, *I* get the key."

"Don't do this," Will said.

His father was now free. Will didn't want him to lose and be a prisoner on the *Dutchman* again.

30

But Bootstrap didn't listen to him and the three men began to play. Very quickly, Bootstrap lost the game.

Jones put the key back inside his shirt. "Bootstrap Bill, you will stay on this ship in my service until the end of time. William Turner … you are free to leave at the next port."

Jones laughed and moved away.

Will was very angry. "Why did you do that?" he asked his father.

Bootstrap dropped his tired head. "I didn't want you to lose," he said sadly.

"The game was never about winning or losing," Will said.

Bootstrap looked at him and then suddenly understood. "The game was about finding the key," he said slowly. "And now you know where it is."

## Chapter 8  The Kraken

Later that night, Bootstrap was on guard when he saw the sails of another ship, the *Edinburgh Trader*. He pointed to the ship.

"Now you can escape," he said to Will.

"Yes," Will replied. "But first I want to get the key."

He moved toward the captain's room and quietly went inside. Jones was asleep. Will took a step closer. Pushing away Jones's beard, he reached for the key. Quickly, he pulled it off its chain.

Will left the room and ran back to Bootstrap.

"Is the ship still there?" he asked.

His eyes searched the ocean for the *Edinburgh Trader*.

"Yes," Bootstrap said. "I've prepared a rowing boat for you, but you must hurry."

Will was very sad to leave his father. "Come with me," he said, as he climbed over the side of the *Dutchman.*.

"I'm part of the ship now, Will. I can't leave. Take this,"

Bootstrap said. He gave Will a black knife from his belt. "I always wanted to give this to you …"

Will smiled. "I'll free you from this prison. I promise you."

Will jumped into the boat and disappeared on the dark water.

The next morning, a large sailor arrived to take Bootstrap's place. The old pirate was asleep and the sailor kicked him hard.

"Move, before the captain sees you."

Suddenly, the sailor saw the white sails of the *Edinburgh Trader*.

"Quickly!" he shouted. "There's a ship near us!"

Davy Jones came out and looked at the ocean.

"Who guarded the ship last night?" he asked angrily.

The sailors pushed Bootstrap forward.

"Didn't you notice that ship?" the captain said.

"Sorry, Captain, I fell asleep. It won't happen again," Bootstrap promised.

"Bring his son to me," Jones ordered.

"He's not on the ship, sir," a sailor said. "And one of the rowing boats is missing."

Jones immediately understood. He looked at Bootstrap and the pirate's face went pale with fear. Jones thought for a minute and then pulled the chain from under his shirt. The key was gone.

"Only one person could plan to steal my key! Jack Sparrow!" he shouted. "Captain Jack Sparrow!"

◆

In the captain's room of the *Edinburgh Trader*, Will was trying to get warm.

"It's strange to find a rowing boat in the middle of the ocean," Captain Bellamy said.

"Just sail the ship away quickly," Will replied. "You have to hurry."

A sailor suddenly ran into the room. "Captain! We've seen a ship!"

"What color are her sails?" Bellamy asked.

"She's not using her sails, sir," the sailor replied.

"Pirates!" Bellamy said.

Will ran out of the room and climbed the mast.

"It's the *Dutchman!*" he shouted. "We're all going to die!"

The *Edinburgh Trader* stopped moving.

"What happened?" one of the sailors asked.

"We've hit something!" another sailor answered.

Captain Bellamy looked into the ocean, but could see nothing.

"Move the ship's wheel left, then right, then left again!" he ordered.

The sailors followed his orders without success, then turned back to their captain.

"What can we do now?" one of them asked.

But Bellamy wasn't there.

The sailors looked out toward the ocean. A large monster was holding the captain in its hand! It lifted Bellamy high into the air, and then pulled him down into the water.

"KRAKEN!" the sailors shouted.

The Kraken killed the captain, then came back for the ship. It broke the ship into two pieces and pulled it down into the ocean.

A few minutes later, six men were on their knees on the *Flying Dutchman*.

"Where is the son?" Jones asked, looking closely at the line of sailors. "And where is the key?"

"We can't find them," Maccus answered. "Maybe the ocean took him."

"I *am* the ocean!" Jones shouted angrily. "Throw these men off the ship."

His men threw the sailors from the *Edinburgh Trader* into the water.

"The chest isn't safe," Jones said. "Bootstrap's son has the key and he's working with Jack Sparrow. We're going to *Isla Cruces.*"

"He won't find the chest," a sailor said.

"He knew about the key, didn't he?" Jones shouted. "He mustn't find the heart. I must reach *Isla Cruces* before Will—or Jack—arrives!"

Below the *Dutchman*, holding onto the side of the ship, Will heard Jones's words.

"Now I know where the chest is hidden," he said to himself. "The *Dutchman* will take me there … and the key is in my pocket!"

◆

Jack was going toward the same island on the *Black Pearl*. His Compass, in Elizabeth's hand, was now working again. But Elizabeth didn't seem to be very happy.

"Elizabeth, are you OK?" Jack asked. "I understand women. I know that something is troubling you."

"I wanted to be married by now," Elizabeth said sadly.

*"I wanted to be married by now."*

She moved away, but Jack followed her.

"You know, I'm a ship's captain. I can marry you here and now."

"No, thank you," Elizabeth said. She wanted to marry Will, not Jack.

"Why not?" he asked her, smiling. "You know that you and I are very similar."

"I'm more honest than you," Elizabeth said. "And I know the difference between right and wrong. And I'm cleaner."

Jack looked at himself. "That's not important!" he said quickly. "You'll soon be like me."

"Do you think so?"

"Yes," Jack said. "You want to be free and selfish. You want to know what that's like. One day," he said, looking into her eyes, "you'll be *exactly* like me."

Elizabeth looked at him coldly. "You and I *are* similar," she agreed. "So one day *you'll* be like *me*. You'll do the right thing. You'll be brave, and then you'll discover a very important fact."

Jack looked at her questioningly.

"You'll discover that you are a good man!" Elizabeth told him, finally.

"I've never done anything good," Jack said.

"I believe that you will. Do you know why? You're going to *want* to be good."

Jack opened his mouth to answer her. A sailor's voice stopped him.

"Land!"

Jack ran to the side of the ship. He could see the small island of *Isla Cruces*, far across the ocean. He looked down into the water.

"The island is too far from here," he said, afraid. "I want my bottle of earth."

# Chapter 9  The Fight for the Chest

Captain Jack Sparrow sat in a rowing boat, holding his bottle of earth. Elizabeth and Norrington were sitting opposite him. Pintel and Ragetti were rowing the boat toward *Isla Cruces*.

"You're rowing too fast," Pintel said to his one-eyed friend.

"You're rowing too slowly," Ragetti answered. "We don't want the Kraken to catch us."

Jack was nervous when he heard the monster's name. Then they heard a sudden noise in the water and the two pirates rowed the boat faster.

When they reached the beach, Jack jumped out of the boat. He checked that the letters were still in his jacket pocket. Then he placed the jacket and the bottle of earth at the end of the boat.

"Guard the boat," he ordered Pintel and Ragetti.

Jack put the Compass into Elizabeth's hands and they walked up the beach. Norrington followed them. They came to an old church.

"Do people live here?" Norrington asked.

"No," Elizabeth answered.

"Do you know this place?" he asked, surprised.

"I've heard stories about it," Elizabeth said. "A religious man came to the island and brought illness and death. All the people died. The man went crazy and killed himself."

Elizabeth looked down at the Compass and continued to walk. Suddenly, the Compass point began to move wildly.

"We've found the place!" she said.

Jack drew an X in the sand with the toe of his boot.

"Make a hole here," he said to Norrington.

At the same time, the *Flying Dutchman* arrived near *Isla Cruces* and Davy Jones noticed the rowing boat.

"They're here," he said angrily. "And I can't step on land again for ten years!"

"Can we do the job for you?" Maccus asked him.

"I'll punish you if you fail!" Jones promised. "Take the ship down below the ocean," he ordered his men.

Maccus called out, "Down, down."

In seconds, the *Flying Dutchman* ship disappeared below the waves and moved toward *Isla Cruces*.

Pintel and Ragetti were sitting on the beach and looking out at the ocean. The water began to move—something was coming toward them! They jumped to their feet. Then they ran to tell Jack.

♦

Jack watched Norrington as he made a deep hole in the sand. Jack was worried and he wanted to find the chest quickly.

Suddenly, Norrington hit something.

"It's the chest!" Jack said and jumped into the hole.

They lifted out the chest and Jack quickly broke open the lock. Inside were a long white dress, dried flowers, and old love letters. Jack pushed them away—and found a box. He lifted the box out of the chest. It was tightly locked, but he could hear a noise inside it.

"The heart!" Elizabeth said. "It's real!"

Norrington was surprised. "You were right," he said to Jack.

"I'm often right," Jack said. "But people are still surprised."

"With good reason," a voice said.

The group turned and saw Will Turner. He was running toward them in wet clothes.

Elizabeth ran to him. "Will—you're all right!" She put her arms around his neck.

Jack looked worried. "How did you get here?" he asked Will.

"With difficulty," Will said. "But I want to thank you, Jack. You tricked me onto that ship—to pay Jones …"

"What?" Elizabeth said, looking at Jack.

"… and then I met my father."

"That's OK," Jack said nervously.

"Everything you said to me … *every word* was untrue?" Elizabeth said. She looked angrily at Jack.

"Yes."

Then the happy smile left Jack's face. Will was on his knees next to the chest. He held the key in one hand, and his father's knife in the other.

"What are you doing?" Jack asked.

"I'm going to kill Jones," Will answered.

In a second, Jack was pressing his sword against Will's neck.

"You can't do that, William," Jack said. "Who will stop the Kraken if Jones is dead? Now, give me the key, please."

Will quickly pushed away Jack's sword. He jumped up and took Elizabeth's sword.

"I keep my promises," he said, facing Jack. "I'm going to free my father."

But suddenly, Norrington pulled out *his* sword and turned to Will. "You can't keep the key. Sorry."

Jack looked at Norrington and smiled. "You're going to help me!" he said, happily.

Norrington pointed his sword quickly toward Jack.

"No," he said. "Lord Beckett wants that chest. He'll make me a commodore again if I give it to him."

The three men began to fight.

"Will," Jack said urgently. "Norrington can't keep the chest! Believe me!"

Will looked at him. "I don't believe anything that you say," he shouted.

"Don't listen to him," Norrington said. "Jack just wants Elizabeth for himself."

The three men jumped back, and continued to fight.

"Guard the chest," Will told Elizabeth.

"No! Adult men *talk* about their problems. They don't fight!" Elizabeth shouted, but the men weren't listening.

Ragetti stood in the trees and watched the fight.

"What's happening?" Pintel asked.

He stood next to Ragetti and they both looked at the chest.

Ragetti tried to explain. "Each man wants the chest. Mr. Norrington hopes to give it to Lord Beckett. Then Beckett will free him. Jack wants to sell the chest to Beckett and save himself. And Turner thinks it will help his cursed old father."

"How sad," Pintel said. "That chest is clearly very important."

He looked at Ragetti, and then the two men walked quietly toward the chest.

Elizabeth fell to the sand and closed her eyes. "Maybe they'll think I'm sick. Then they'll stop fighting," she thought.

She didn't move for a long time. When she opened her eyes, she saw Pintel and Ragetti. They were running away with the chest.

*They were running away with the chest.*

She jumped to her feet.

"Shall I tell Will or follow the chest?" she asked herself.

The three men were still fighting. She decided to follow the chest.

## Chapter 10 Jack's Big Mistake

The three men were moving across the island as they fought. Norrington pushed Will hard and he dropped the key. It flew through the air and fell into Jack's hand.

"Hah-hah!" Jack screamed.

He ran away down the beach. Norrington and Will quickly followed him.

Holding the key tightly, Jack went into the old church and climbed some wooden stairs. High above him, the bones of the old churchman hung from a chain.

Jack said "Hello" to him and continued his climb.

Norrington and Will quickly followed Jack up the stairs. Norrington attacked Jack with his sword, but Jack stepped away. Norrington ran at him, took the key, and threw Jack down the stairs.

As Jack fell, his hand found the dead churchman's chain. Jack and the churchman dropped down together.

At the same time Will, holding onto a second chain, was pulled up toward Norrington. As he passed the commodore, he took the key. Then he ran out onto the church roof.

♦

On the beach, the water started to move again. Slowly, the heads of Jones's sailors came up out of the pale blue water. The men walked across the beach and stood next to the empty hole.

Then they saw Will Turner step out onto the church roof.

Will was trying to escape from Jack, Norrington—and now from Jones's men. He jumped across a hole in the roof. Using the point of his sword, Norrington lifted the key from Will's hand. The commodore held it for a second—then it disappeared. Jack had it again!

Norrington turned angrily and knocked Jack's sword from his hand. He looked over his shoulder at Will.

"Excuse me," he said. "I'm going to kill the man who destroyed my life."

"That's OK," Will answered.

Jack held up one finger. "Let's talk about this, Commodore. Are you sure you have the right man?"

Will smiled. Jack was trying to save himself again.

"You caught a famous pirate and put him in prison," Jack said. "You wanted to marry a beautiful woman. Who freed the pirate and stole your girl?"

Jack turned toward Will.

Norrington stopped Jack.

"You've said enough!" he shouted and pushed his sword wildly at Jack.

Jack threw up his hands and screamed. He fell down the roof and the key dropped to the ground.

"Good work!" Will said.

"But sadly, Mr. Turner, he was right," Norrington said.

He turned his sword toward Will. Norrington hated Jack, but he didn't like Will, either.

Down on the ground, Jack picked up the key and ran.

"I'm on your side, friend!" he called up to Will.

Jack slowed to a walk and put the key around his neck.

"I'm safe now," he said to himself.

Then he fell into a hole in the ground.

Will jumped onto a large wooden water wheel on the side of the church. Norrington jumped on, too. With a loud noise, the

*Will jumped onto a large wooden water wheel on the side of the church. Norrington jumped on, too.*

wheel suddenly broke away from the wall. It began to move across the ground with the two men on top of it.

Jack was hit by the wheel when he finally pulled himself out of the hole. The key fell away from his neck and caught on the wheel.

"I've lost the key … again!" he said.

He started to run after the wheel.

♦

Elizabeth finally reached Pintel and Ragetti in the trees.

"Hello, love," Pintel said, and smiled.

He and Ragetti put down the chest and pulled out their swords. Elizabeth reached for her sword, but it wasn't in her belt. Will had it, she suddenly remembered.

The two pirates attacked her, but suddenly something crashed through the trees. They turned and saw the water wheel. Jack was running behind it.

Pintel and Ragetti turned back to Elizabeth, but then a knife hit a tree next to Ragetti's head. Jones's men were coming!

Pintel and Ragetti dropped their swords at Elizabeth's feet, took the chest, and started to run. With a sword in each hand, Elizabeth ran through the trees behind them.

The pirates tried to run around a tree, one each side of it, but they were holding the chest between them. As they stopped, Jones's men arrived.

Ragetti, Pintel, and Elizabeth looked at the chest, and then at the terrible sailors. They all made the quick decision to leave the chest on the ground.

♦

On another part of the island, Jack was still running after the wheel and the key. He ran quickly, got close to the wheel, and jumped inside it.

Will reached down from the top of the wheel. He took the key before Jack could. Then he also jumped inside the wheel. Norrington followed him quickly.

Cutting Will with his sword, Jack took the key again. He climbed on top of the wheel, and then jumped into a tree.

Hanging from the tree, Jack noticed one of Jones's sailors. He was coming toward the tree—and he was carrying the chest! Jack reached for a piece of wood and threw it at the sailor's head.

The wood knocked the undead sailor's head off his shoulders. Jack jumped out of the tree and looked around. He couldn't see anybody. With the key in hand, he carefully walked up to the chest.

Jack sat down next to the chest, and turned the key in the lock. And there it was—Jones's heart. Taking off his shirt, he put the heart inside it. Then he looked around again. Nobody was watching him.

He ran straight to the rowing boat and found his bottle. It was large enough and had a wide top … He emptied some of the earth onto the beach, and placed the covered heart inside the bottle. Then he filled the bottle with sand.

He looked up when he heard a sudden noise. Pintel, Ragetti, and Elizabeth ran out of the trees. The two men were carrying the chest again, and Jones's sailors were close behind them.

Elizabeth fought Jones's men bravely, but she was losing the fight. Then the big wheel crashed out of the trees and knocked down some of Jones's men. Elizabeth escaped to Pintel and Ragetti, and they pulled the chest through the sand toward the rowing boat.

Jack was unhappy. There were too many people on the beach. He put his bottle back into the end of the rowing boat and watched.

The wheel finally stopped near the water, and Will and Norrington climbed out. Norrington fell into the rowing boat. He lifted his head, saw Jack's bottle, and reached toward it. Jack watched carefully. Then Norrington's hand moved past the bottle and reached for the letters in Jack's coat pocket. Jack didn't stop him because he didn't need the papers now. He had the heart. Davy Jones and every ship on the ocean were his.

The fight on the beach between Sparrow's men and Jones's men continued.

Suddenly, Will noticed the chest. The key was in the lock and he started to open it. Jack quickly turned around and hit him, and Will fell. Elizabeth ran to his side and looked down at him.

"We're not going to escape," she said to Norrington.

"Not with the chest," he replied. He quickly took the chest

and ordered her into the boat. "Don't wait for me," he called, as he disappeared from the beach into the trees.

Jones's men followed him.

"We must listen to him," Jack said quickly.

"Yes!" Pintel agreed and pushed the rowing boat into the water.

Jack picked up his bottle. With the heart and Tia Dalma's earth inside it, he was safe.

"We have to take Will," Elizabeth ordered.

Jack looked angry but agreed. Pintel and Ragetti pulled Will into the boat. Without another word, they left the island—and Norrington—behind.


## Chapter 11  The End of Captain Jack?

Jack's men were soon back on the *Black Pearl*. Will slowly opened his eyes.

"What happened to the chest?" he asked.

"Norrington took it. Jones's men followed him," Elizabeth told him.

Gibbs came and welcomed them all onto the ship. He was ready to sail.

"Jack!" he said. "We saw the *Dutchman* an hour ago. She was coming around the end of the island!"

"Was she?" Jack replied. He didn't seem worried.

"The most dangerous ship on the ocean is too close to us!" Gibbs called to the other sailors. "Pull up the sails!"

Jack felt no need to hurry. He sat down and held his bottle tightly to him.

"Gibbs, is your mouth dry?" he asked. "Is your heart moving quickly in your chest?"

"Yes," Gibbs answered.

"I think you're afraid," Jack told him.

"Well, aren't you afraid, too?" Gibbs said. He didn't understand Jack. Where was the frightened captain of only a few hours before?

Elizabeth walked across the ship to the two men. She agreed with Jack.

"We're in no danger," she said to Gibbs. "I can't see any ships."

She spoke too quickly. As they watched, the ocean began to move. Suddenly, the *Flying Dutchman* came up from below the water and stopped next to the *Pearl*.

Jack turned toward the *Dutchman* and lifted the bottle above his head. He pointed to it, smiled, and gave a friendly wave.

On the *Dutchman*, Davy Jones realized what he meant. "He's got my heart!" He turned to Maccus. "Prepare the guns," he said.

"We're here! Yoo-hoo! Let's talk!" Jack shouted.

"What are you doing?" Gibbs asked angrily.

"Be quiet," Jack replied. He lifted the bottle again. "I have the heart. In here," he said quietly.

"Really? How?" Gibbs asked.

Jack smiled. "I'm Captain Jack Sparrow, remember? Nobody is smarter than me."

Gibbs knew very well that Jack wasn't always right.

"I have to protect the ship," he said, and shouted, "Move to the left! Hurry, men!"

The *Black Pearl* sailed away from the *Dutchman*. The *Dutchman's* guns began to shoot but the *Pearl* was escaping.

"Can the *Black Pearl* move faster than the *Dutchman*?" Will asked.

"That isn't a natural ship," Gibbs said, pointing to the *Flying Dutchman*. "It can sail into the wind, and not lose speed. That's how it catches other ships. But if the wind is behind us—"

"We can move faster than her!" Will said. Suddenly, he understood Gibbs's plan.

"Yes," Gibbs said. "The *Black Pearl* is the only ship that Davy Jones fears."

Jack smiled, and held his bottle close to his chest.

"We can take the *Dutchman*!" Will said to Jack. "We can turn and fight!"

"Or we can run away," Jack answered brightly.

"You have the only ship that can take the *Dutchman* in a fair fight."

"But I don't like to fight fairly," Jack said.

Suddenly, the *Black Pearl* moved to one side and sailors fell to the floor. Jack's bottle was knocked from his hands and broke. Sand and earth went everywhere. Jack fell to his knees and looked through it. There was nothing in there except sand.

Jack looked up at Gibbs. "Um … I don't have the heart."

"Then who does?" Gibbs asked.

Jack turned pale. He didn't have Jones's heart, and he didn't have Tia Dalma's earth.

The *Pearl* stopped moving and Elizabeth looked out at the ocean.

"Have we hit some rocks?" she called.

"I heard those words on the *Edinburgh Trader*," remembered Will. "No!" he shouted. "It's not rocks! Move back!"

"What is it?" Elizabeth asked, seeing the fear in Will's eyes.

"The Kraken," Gibbs said. "It's coming for Jack."

The men on the *Pearl* were silent.

Jack stopped looking through the sand on the floor of the ship. The heart wasn't there, and the black mark was on his hand again.

Very quietly, Jack moved toward the end of the *Pearl*. None of his men saw him climb into a small boat. He rowed quickly away from his ship.

The water around the *Pearl* began to move as, slowly, the Kraken came up out of the ocean.

"Go to the guns!" Will shouted. "Protect the ship."

The pirates quickly prepared for the monster's attack.

The Kraken's long arms moved onto the ship, but the guns were ready. Will ordered the men to shoot the monster.

Badly hurt, the Kraken moved away. It broke all the ship's small rowing boats as it went down.

"It will return!" Will shouted. Turning to Elizabeth he said, "Get off the ship."

"There are no boats," Elizabeth replied. "The Kraken destroyed all of them."

Not all of them …

As the Kraken prepared to attack again, Jack rowed away more quickly. But something stopped his escape. When he looked down at his Compass, it was pointing toward the *Black Pearl* and his men.

Sadly, Jack began to row back again.

On the *Pearl*, the Kraken was winning the fight. The pirates shot at it repeatedly, but they couldn't stop it.

Elizabeth stood in the captain's room, with a gun in her shaking hands. She was very angry. "Jack has disappeared," she said to herself. "*He's* the person that the Kraken wants. *He* brought us into this mess."

Then, as the Kraken's arms moved slowly through the windows toward her, she dropped the gun. She ran up to the top of the ship—and into Jack. He was back.

"We have some time. Leave the ship!" he ordered.

"Can we really escape in a rowing boat?" Will asked.

"We can return to the island. We can escape while the Kraken takes down the *Pearl*." Jack's eyes showed his sadness at the thought of the end of his ship.

Will, Gibbs, and the other pirates went toward the rowing boat.

"Thank you, Jack," Elizabeth said softly. She moved closer to him. "You came back. I always knew that you were a good man."

She kissed the pirate, then stepped back slowly. There was a sharp noise.

Jack looked down at his hands.

"I've chained you to the side of the *Pearl*," Elizabeth explained. "The Kraken wants you—not the ship, and not us."

"You're a great pirate," Jack said.

Elizabeth looked at him for the last time and remembered—so much, and so many adventures. Then she ran off the ship and left Jack … waiting.

Slowly, the Kraken's arms moved onto the *Pearl*, and the monster's head moved toward Jack. Its mouth was open and in its teeth was Jack's lost, much-loved hat. He took it out of the monster's mouth and placed it on his head.

"Hello, monster," he said.

From the rowing boat, the pirates of the *Black Pearl* watched the Kraken and Jack fight. Slowly, the terrible monster covered the ship with its body. Then it pulled the ship, and Jack, down below the waves.

Davy Jones stood on the *Flying Dutchman* and smiled. "Jack Sparrow," he said happily. "Now I have you."

Jones was not the only person watching from the *Dutchman*. As Jack went down with the ship, Bootstrap Bill watched the water, too. Sadly, he remembered Jack Sparrow—Captain Jack Sparrow.

"I thought you could do it," he said quietly. "Only you."

The *Black Pearl* and her captain were gone. And, already, the world seemed a darker place without them.

# ACTIVITIES

## Chapters 1–2

*Before you read*

1  Look at the Word List at the back of this book. Check the meanings of words that are new to you. Then use some of the words in the sentences below.

   **a** The police … the thief.

   **b** We … a small boat from the ship to the beach.

   **c** He hid the money in a strong, wooden … .

   **d** The ship sailed into the … .

   **e** A sharp … can kill somebody.

   **f** The … was the most important man on the island.

   **g** The tallest part of a ship is the … .

   **h** The men searched for hidden … .

   **i** … are thieves who sail the oceans.

   **j** He hung the key on a … around his neck.

2  Discuss these questions with other students.

   **a** What is the Caribbean? How many Caribbean islands can you name?

   **b** What do you know about pirates? How did they get money? Are there any pirates in the world today?

   **c** Do you know about anybody who has found treasure in your country? What was it and where is the treasure now?

3  Read the Introduction. Which people from the first *Pirates of the Caribbean* story will you read about again in *Dead Man's Chest*? Look through this book and find pictures of them. What do you think will happen to them?

*While you read*

4  What are these people and places called?

   **a** the captain of the *Black Pearl*          ...........................

   **b** the fine old pirate on the *Black Pearl*   ...........................

   **c** the pirate with no teeth                   ...........................

   **d** the town where Elizabeth lives             ...........................

   **e** the man that Elizabeth wants to marry      ...........................

   **f** Elizabeth's father                         ...........................

50

| **g** | Will's father | ............................. |
| **h** | the captain of the *Flying Dutchman* | ............................. |
| **i** | the man who wants Jack's Compass | ............................. |
| **j** | the dirtiest port in the Caribbean | ............................. |

*After you read*

**5** Answer these questions.

    **a** Where does Jack Sparrow escape from?

    **b** Where does he go to?

    **c** What is unusual about the monkey?

    **d** What is Jack Sparrow searching for?

    **e** Why is Will late for his wedding?

    **f** Why does Beckett arrest Elizabeth and Will?

    **g** Why is the black mark on Jack's hand dangerous?

    **h** Who does the Kraken work for?

    **i** Two men find Jack's hat. What happens to them?

**6** Imagine that you are Elizabeth. Answer these questions.

    **a** What do you feel about Will?

    **b** Why are you angry with Lord Beckett?

    **c** Your father wants you to leave Port Royal. Why don't you want to go?

    **d** Why do you take Lord Beckett's letters?

    **e** Why do you sail on the *Edinburgh Trader*?

## Chapters 3–4

*Before you read*

**7** Discuss these people in the story with other students.

    **a** Captain Jack Sparrow:

        Is he a brave man? Do you like him? Why (not)? Who is he afraid of? What does he want to find and why?

    **b** Will Turner:

        What is his plan? Where is he at the end of Chapter 2? What will happen to him next?

    **c** Elizabeth Swann:

        Why is she wearing sailor's clothes at the end of Chapter 2? What will she do next?

**8** Are these sentences right (✔) or wrong (✗)?

   **a** Will Turner is a prisoner of the Pelegostos.    .....

   **b** There are animal bones around Jack's chair.    .....

   **c** The Pelegostos put Will in a cage.    .....

   **d** The Pelegostos want to cook and eat Jack.    .....

   **e** Will and the pirates leave Jack on the island.    .....

   **f** Elizabeth is going to Tortuga on the *Black Pearl*.    .....

   **g** The pirates visit Tia Dalma.    .....

   **h** Davy Jones's heart is inside the chest.    .....

   **i** Tia Dalma gives Jack a bottle of earth.    .....

   **j** Davy Jones's ship is called the *Edinburgh Trader*.    .....

*After you read*

**9** Who is speaking? Who to? What are they talking about?

   **a** "Tell them to free me."

   **b** "She is going to die."

   **c** "It's ours!"

   **d** "Why don't you watch her more carefully?"

   **e** "It's terrible— it can pull a ship to the bottom of the ocean."

   **f** "I will pay you with this."

   **g** "A man of the ocean, a great sailor …"

   **h** "If you don't want it, give it back to me."

   **i** "We need to find Davy Jones and the *Flying Dutchman*."

**10** Work with another student.

   *Student A*: You are Jack Sparrow and you want Tia Dalma's help. Ask her questions about Davy Jones, the key, and the chest. Can she give you anything more than information?

   *Student B*: You are Tia Dalma. Answer Jack's questions and tell him Davy Jones's story. Explain why Davy Jones cut his heart from his body. Tell Jack why the chest is important. Offer him more help—for payment.

## Chapters 5–6

*Before you read*

**11** Guess what happens in the next part of the book.

    **a** Who will Will meet on the *Flying Dutchman*?

        Elizabeth   Jack Sparrow   Pintel and Ragetti

    **b** Who will become Davy Jones's prisoner?

        Will Turner   Elizabeth   Jack Sparrow

    **c** Who will Jack and Elizabeth meet in Tortuga?

        Governor Swann   Commodore Norrington   Davy Jones

*While you read*

**12** Circle the correct answers.

    **a** Who goes to search the old ship?

        Jack Sparrow   Will   Gibbs

    **b** On which part of the dead sailor's body does Will see red marks?

        on his arm   on his chest   on his back

    **c** Which ship comes up from the bottom of the ocean?

        the *Flying Dutchman*   the *Edinburgh Trader*   the *Black Pearl*

    **d** For how many years was Jack Sparrow captain of the *Black Pearl*?

        twelve   thirteen   fourteen

    **e** How many souls does Davy Jones want?

        four   fifty   one hundred

    **f** Where does Jack meet Norrington?

        Port Royal   Isla de Muerta   Tortuga

    **g** Who helps Jack find new sailors for the *Black Pearl*?

        Will Turner   Elizabeth   Gibbs

    **h** Who takes Norrington away from the bar?

        Elizabeth   Will Turner   Gibbs

    **i** What does Jack place in Elizabeth's hand?

        a key   the Compass   a sword

    **j** What is inside the chest?

        a heart   a sword   treasure

*After you read*

13 Complete each sentence with words on the right.

    **a** Will goes to the old ship     **from** the bottom of the

    **b** The old ship won't move     ocean.

    **c** The *Flying Dutchman*     **to** find the key to the chest.

    comes up     **for** Jack Sparrow's soul.

    **d** Will stops fighting     **to** find ninety-nine souls.

    **e** Jones wants one     **from** this world to the next.

    hundred souls     **because** the water is too

    **f** Jack and Gibbs go to     shallow.

    Tortuga     **when** someone hits him.

    **g** Gibbs is surprised     **that** Norrington is now a

    **h** The *Flying Dutchman*     rough pirate.

    takes dead men

14 Imagine that you are Norrington. Talk about yourself. Why are you in Tortuga? Why do you want to join the *Black Pearl*? Why do you want to kill Jack Sparrow? Why do you hate him?

**Chapters 7–9**

*Before you read*

15 Look at the titles of the next three chapters. What do you think is going to happen? Discuss the questions.

*Chapter 7 A Very Important Game*

The game is played on the *Flying Dutchman*. Who plays? What do they hope to win?

*Chapter 8 The Kraken*

Who will the Kraken kill next?

*Chapter 9 The Fight for the Chest*

Three people fight for the chest. Who are they?

*While you read*

16 Circle the correct word(s).

    **a** Davy Jones plays *the piano* / *football*.

    **b** Will meets his *brother* / *father* on the Flying Dutchman.

    **c** Will offers Davy Jones one *hundred* / *thousand* years of service on the *Flying Dutchman*.

   **d**   Will is very *sad / happy* when he leaves his father.

   **e**   Will steals the *chest / key* from Davy Jones.

   **f**   Jack's Compass works when *Elizabeth / Norrington* holds it.

   **g**   Jack offers to *kill / marry* Elizabeth.

   **h**   Davy Jones cannot step on land for *ten / twenty* years.

   **i**   Norrington makes a hole in the sand and finds *treasure / a chest.*

   **j**   Pintel and Ragetti steal the *chest / key*.

*After you read*

**17**  Complete these sentences.

   **a**   Bootstrap Bill helps Will because …

   **b**   Will wants to play the numbers game to …

   **c**   Will goes to Davy Jones's room to …

   **d**   The sailors on the *Edinburgh Trader* are afraid when …

   **e**   Jack wants his bottle of earth because …

   **f**   When the religious man came to *Isla Cruces*, he …

**18**  Work with two other students. Have this conversation.

   *Student A*:  You are Jack and you want the chest. Explain your reasons to Norrington and Will.

   *Student B*:  You are Will. You want the chest, too. Explain your reasons to Jack and Norrington.

   *Student C*:  You are Norrington. Explain why you also want the chest.

**19**  Look at the picture on page 39.

   **a**   Who are these men?

   **b**   What part have they played in the story?

   **c**   Do you think they will be able to keep the chest?

## Chapters 10–11

*Before you read*

**20**  How will this story end? Who will get the chest? Will Captain Jack Sparrow live or die? Discuss your ideas with another student.

*While you read*

**21** Put these sentences in the right order. Number them 1–8.

  **a** The *Flying Dutchman* attacks the *Black Pearl*. .....

  **b** Elizabeth meets Pintel and Ragetti. .....

  **c** Jones's men arrive on the island. .....

  **d** The Kraken pulls Jack Sparrow into the ocean. .....

  **e** Jack opens the chest and takes the heart. .....

  **f** Elizabeth, Will, and Jack leave Norrington on the island. .....

  **g** Jack, Will, and Norrington fight. .....

  **h** The Kraken attacks the *Black Pearl*. .....

*After you read*

**22** Discuss why these things are important in the story.

  **a** a bottle of earth

  **b** Davy Jones's heart

  **c** Jack's hat

  **d** the Kraken

**23** Work with another student.

  *Student A:* You are Elizabeth and you are on the *Black Pearl*. You see the Kraken pull Captain Jack Sparrow below the waves. How do you feel? Where will you go next? Who will you go with?

  *Student B:* You are Will Turner. Talk to Elizabeth about Captain Jack. Did you like him? Why (not)? What will you do next?

**24** Do you like the ending of this story? Why (not)? Can you think of a different one?

**Writing**

**25** Imagine that you are a pirate in Tortuga. You want to join the *Black Pearl*. Write a letter to Captain Jack Sparrow and give your reasons.

**26** Write a conversation between Will and Tia Dalma after the end of the story. What can Tia Dalma see in the future for Will, Elizabeth—and Captain Jack Sparrow?

27 You are Davy Jones. You cut out your heart and put it in the dead man's chest. Explain your actions in a short letter to the woman you loved.

28 Write a conversation between Elizabeth Swann and a friend in Tortuga. Elizabeth is telling a friend about her love for Will Turner and her escape from Port Royal.

29 Find out more about a real pirate and write about him. Describe when and where he lived, his activities, and his death.

30 You are Lord Beckett. You want to catch Captain Jack Sparrow—dead or alive. Offer money, through a newspaper, to anyone who brings the pirate to you.

31 You work for the Tortuga Tourist Office. Write about the island, and its port, for a British magazine. Tell people why they should visit the island.

32 You are a newspaper reporter in the Caribbean. You have heard about the Kraken. Write about it for your newspaper.

33 Tell the story of this book. Did you enjoy it? Why (not)? Write about it for your friends.

34 Write your own short story about pirates searching for treasure.

# WORD LIST

**arrest** (n/v) the act of taking someone to a police station or prison after a crime

**bone** (n) one of the hard parts that form your body

**cage** (n) a large box made of thin pieces of metal or wood, usually for birds or animals

**captain** (n) the most important officer on a ship. A **commodore** is an even more important officer, with many people and ships below him

**chain** (n/v) a line of metal rings that are joined together

**chest** (n) a large, strong box that you keep things in

**compass** (n) something that shows north, south, east, and west

**curse** (n/v) words that are meant to bring someone bad luck

**governor** (n) the most important government officer in a place; a governor acts for a king, queen, or president

**Lord** (n) the title of an upper-class British man

**mark** (n/v) a small dark or dirty area on something

**mast** (n) a tall piece of wood that holds up the sails of a ship

**monkey** (n) a small brown animal with a long tail that climbs trees with its hands and tail

**monster** (n) a large, ugly, dangerous animal in stories

**pirate** (n) a sailor who steals from other boats

**port** (n) a safe area for ships; a town where ships can take on people or things

**row** (v) to move a boat across water, using two long pieces of wood with flat ends

**soul** (n) the part of a person that continues to exist after death

**sword** (n) a long piece of metal with sharp sides used for fighting

**treasure** (n) wonderful things like gold and silver. Treasure is often hidden to keep it safe